W9-DJE-119

CREEPY CRAWLIES

Millipedes

by Kari Schuetz

BELLWETHER MEDIA • MINNEAPOLIS, MN

Note to Librarians, Teachers, and Parents:

Blastoff! Readers are carefully developed by literacy experts and combine standards-based content with developmentally appropriate text.

Level 1 provides the most support through repetition of high-frequency words, light text, predictable sentence patterns, and strong visual support.

Level 2 offers early readers a bit more challenge through varied simple sentences, increased text load, and less repetition of high-frequency words.

Level 3 advances early-fluent readers toward fluency through increased text and concept load, less reliance on visuals, longer sentences, and more literary language.

Level 4 builds reading stamina by providing more text per page, increased use of punctuation, greater variation in sentence patterns, and increasingly challenging vocabulary.

Level 5 encourages children to move from "learning to read" to "reading to learn" by providing even more text, varied writing styles, and less familiar topics.

Whichever book is right for your reader, Blastoff! Readers are the perfect books to build confidence and encourage a love of reading that will last a lifetime!

This edition first published in 2016 by Bellwether Media, Inc.

No part of this publication may be reproduced in whole or in part without written permission of the publisher. For information regarding permission, write to Bellwether Media, Inc., Attention: Permissions Department, 5357 Penn Avenue South, Minneapolis, MN 55419.

Library of Congress Cataloging-in-Publication Data

Schuetz, Kari, author.
  Millipedes / by Kari Schuetz.
    pages cm – (Blastoff! Readers. Creepy Crawlies)
  Summary: "Developed by literacy experts for students in kindergarten through grade three, this book introduces millipedes to young readers through leveled text and related photos"– Provided by publisher.
  Audience: Ages 5-8
  Audience: K to grade 3
  Includes bibliographical references and index.
  ISBN 978-1-62617-225-8 (hardcover: alk. paper)
  1. Millipedes–Juvenile literature. I. Title.
  QL449.6.S38 2016
  595.6'6–dc23
                        2015005967

Printed in the United States of America, North Mankato, MN.

Table of Contents

Slow Movers

Millipedes are **arthropods** with lots of legs.

They are born with only six legs. Then they grow more pairs.

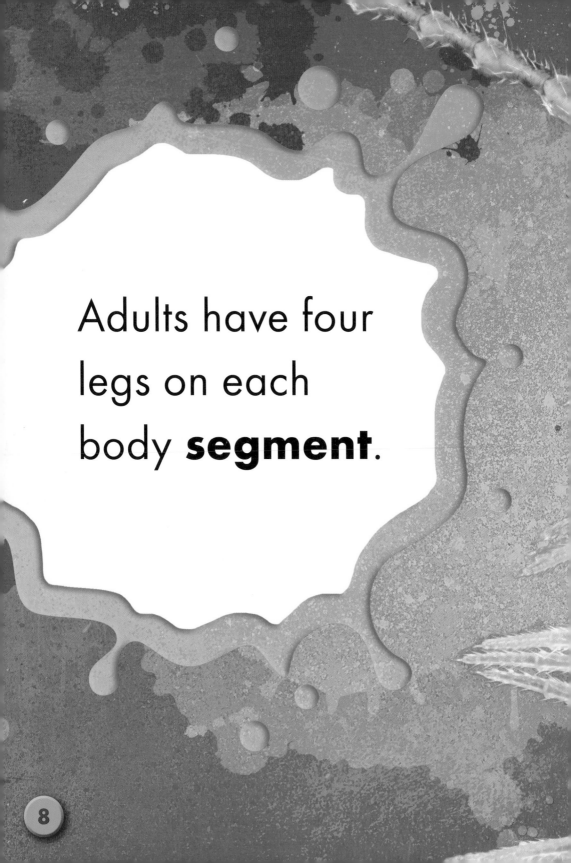

Adults have four legs on each body **segment**.

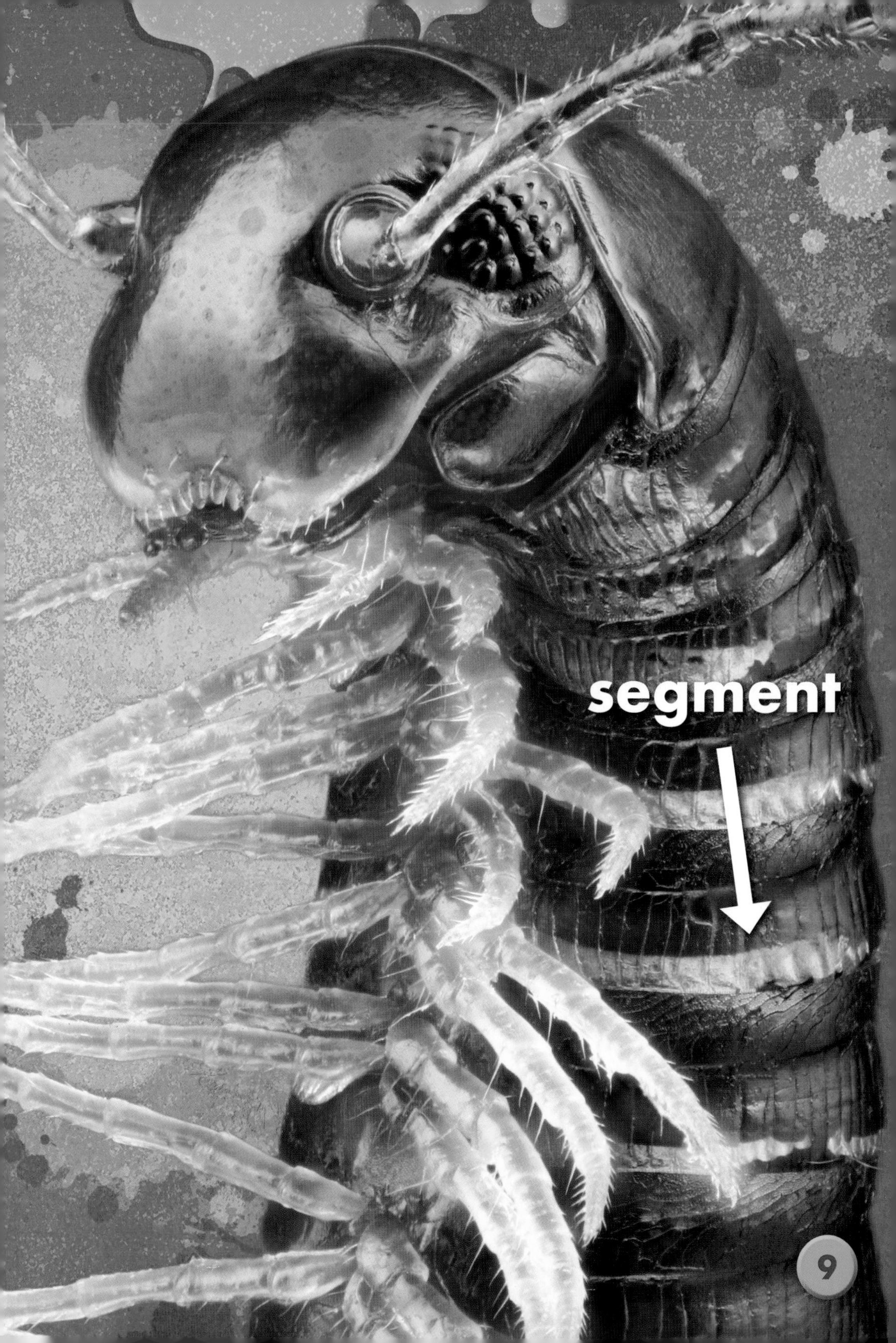
segment

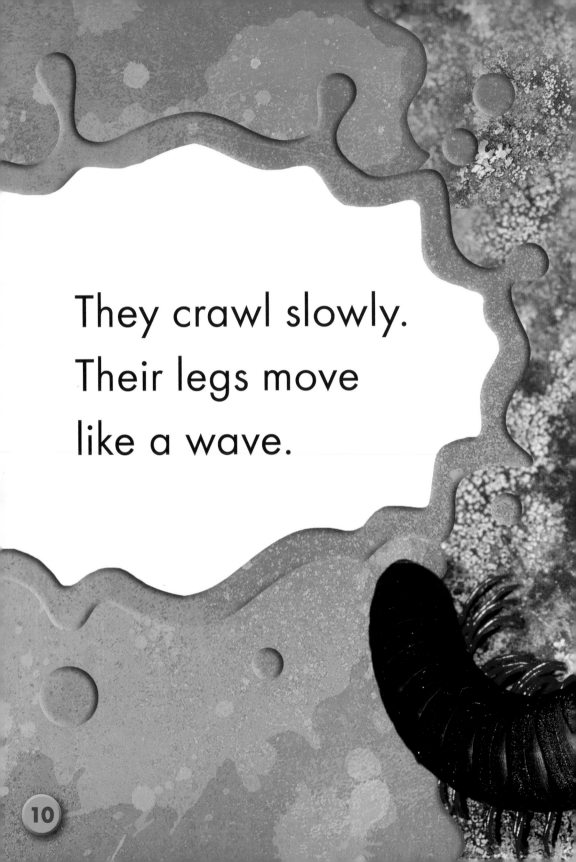

They crawl slowly.
Their legs move
like a wave.

In the Soil

Millipedes like **damp** places. They often stay in soil under rocks and leaves.

They eat plants and dead leaves. Large millipedes even eat **insects**.

Facing Danger

Birds, foxes, and other **predators** hunt millipedes.

Sometimes millipedes curl up to stay safe.

Other times they squirt a gross liquid. Get away, tortoise!

Glossary

arthropods—small animals, such as insects and spiders, that have divided bodies

damp—a little bit wet

insects—small animals with six legs and hard outer bodies; an insect's body is divided into three parts.

predators—animals that hunt other animals for food

segment—a part or division

To Learn More

AT THE LIBRARY

Arlon, Penelope. *Bugs*. New York, N.Y.: Dorling Kindersley, 2011.

Lawton, Caroline. *Bugs A to Z*. New York, N.Y.: Scholastic, 2011.

Schuetz, Kari. *Centipedes*. Minneapolis, Minn.: Bellwether Media, 2016.

ON THE WEB

Learning more about millipedes is as easy as 1, 2, 3.

1. Go to www.factsurfer.com.

2. Enter "millipedes" into the search box.

3. Click the "Surf" button and you will see a list of related web sites.

With factsurfer.com, finding more information is just a click away.

Index

The images in this book are reproduced through the courtesy of: Sakdinon Kadchiangsaen, front cover; Matthew Cole, p. 5; Ardea/ Steve Hopkins/ Animals Animals, p. 7; Matthias Lenke/ SuperStock, p. 9; Thomas Marent/ Minden Pictures/ Corbis, p. 11; style_TTT, p. 13; Jonathan Knott/ Alamy, p. 15; Erwin Niemand, p. 17; Komkrit Preechacanwate, p. 19; Anthony Bannister/ Gallo Images/ Corbis, p. 21.